If the WALLS Could Talk:
8 Strategies to Release **YOUR VISION**
with Passion & Purpose

Thank You for supporting my Vision & Passion! -nb

the 168™ life

Chronicles of a Serial Entrepreneur Series

Book 1

If the WALLS Could Talk:
8 Strategies to release YOUR VISION with Passion & Purpose

Nicholas "Nick" Bartley, M.Ed

VISION②LIFE
PUBLISHING

The 168 Life Project
2015

First Printing: 2016

ISBN: 978-0-692-63812-5

Vision 2 Life Publishing
The V2L Corporation, LLC
P O Box 115112
Atlanta, GA 30310

www.V2Lpublishing.com

Ordering Information: Visit www.The168Life.com

Special discounts are available on quantity purchases by corporations, associations, educators, and bulk orders. For details, contact the publisher via email at: **books@The168Life.com**

U.S. trade bookstores/wholesalers:

Please contact The V2L Corporation, LLC

Tel: (404) 913-6825

Email: info@V2Lcorporation.com

Dedication

To my AWESOME supporters...Thank You. Without your support and patience, WE would have never achieved this milestone.

Time Capsule:
February 23, 2041 ... The 25th Anniversary of this book will be a Conference & Celebration of those coming together to share, inspire, and motivate others... Theme: Your VISION Will Not Die!

Contents

Acknowledgements

I would like to thank all who supported this project with time, comments, encouragement, and especially financially. Without your assistance, this book would never have been completed.

I wanted to give an eternal "Thank You" to all who pre-ordered, which for some was well over a year and a half when the project first launched, for your patience and support in the production of this project and for believing in me enough to support financially.

Nicholas "Nick" Bartley (Me, for not giving up)
Barbara A. Bartley (Mother and #1 supporter & cheerleader)
Laura Daniels (Grandmother and other #1 biggest supporter)
Anthony & Gwennette Watson (MY Pastors & Spiritual covering)
Kimberly Sewell (My BPF and Ultimate supporter & coach)

The EntreSphere: Major Contributors, Promoters & Donors

Career Magazine
Jacqueline Averett
Valeria Clark
Johnny & Flecia Cooke
Veronica Dugger
Naeemah Jade
Adrienne Latimer

Onte McClendon
Demondrae McDowell
Andrae & Shalonda Orr
Brenda Slaughter
Al Sneed
Robert & Virginia Williams
Michael Wilson

PreOrder Book Purchasers and The 168 Life Campaign Supporters

Vinson Allen
Demonica Banks.
Ronquavias Banks
Chris & Mariolina Bartley
Jerry Bartley
Joseph Bartley
Kenneth Bartley
Laura Bartley
Corey Braxton
Gail Brown
Tina Brown
Dora Charles
Eugenie Charles
Natasha Davis

Orane Douglas
Jackie Dugger
Nedra Ellis
Zandra Everett
Jamal Grooms
LaVetta Hudson
Rosa Hunt
Yolanda Johnson
Lillian Jones
Hiawatha/Shameka Lane
Desiree Lee
Deborah Little
Elijah Lowe
Bob Mackey

Chris & Chanel Martin
Shadeequa Miller
Brian & Denise Miller
Jermaine Newman
Ray & Rita Nobles
Damian/Tiffany Pearson
Joseph Raby
Kimisha Semien
Lydell Smith
Harvey Watson, Jr.
Patrick & Selisa Watson
Stephanie Whitehurst
Jonathan Wigfall
Keysha Wilson

Preface

As the old saying goes, "If these walls could talk, oh the stories, secrets, and more they would tell." Imagine the walls that surround many successful people and brands that started out with an entrepreneurial vision in the living room, bathroom, or even during someone's lunch break at their "job". Those walls are encrypted with information that has become company secrets. They have witnessed moments of anxiety, they are marked with joys of milestone celebrations, and they continue to shield and protect as the vision continues to transpire into what it was divinely created to do. This book is going to use these walls to serve as your virtual coach to guide you through this journey. Sometimes, in order for God to birth out million dollar ideas we have to endure the test and trials in solitude as to not allow anyone to taint or infect the Vision during delivery. The walls are all we have as we stare at them for insight, lean against them for balance and leverage, place things on them for safe keeping, or to contain ourselves within them for protection.

This book is intended to awaken a dormant spirit from within that was implanted before the notion of our conception. If the Walls Could Talk, they would tell you that my experiences in life and during my entrepreneurial journey were designed specifically for me, yet, they would tell me the journey comes with a road map. Despite "how" successful business owners arrived to their destinations, they would agree that the foundation has to be solid and there are key strategies that one must take into consideration if they desire to achieve the goals they set out to accomplish. Therefore, I take pride in having this opportunity to share my story for the sole purpose of assisting individuals who know they have a vision for success in their many endeavors, but the fear, lack of resources, or lack of knowledge has reduced that vision to merely a hopeful dream. Well we are about to change that mindset TODAY and RIGHT NOW. I must first say this book is not some fairy tale of how I made a smooth transition from college to working a professional career to launching a successful business as I followed my passion in pursuit of fulfilling my dreams; it will tell you the process and journey I went through to understand the purpose as to what God has called me to be, so that I might share it to help many others get where they have been appointed to be. There is no sugar coating and carefully crafting of words because when the walls begin to talk, they just "keep it real" and let you know how it is and give you a pep talk to make sure your head is in the game.

As I dedicate this project to the celebration of a 5 year milestone, I know that it is grace and favor that have sustained me for this period of time without the assistance of traditional employment. Doors have been opened to provide in times of need at their duly appointed times and the rest was up to me to work the vision, share the blessings, give praise, and repeat that cycle. As you read these words, I encourage you to pray for God's discernment in relation to your vision. May these words bring clarity and evoke a boldness to walk out on faith, but with the knowledge to operate in order and excellence. Therefore, I share these 8 strategies to release your VISION with passion and purpose to catapult you to success. Keep in mind this book isn't just for you to read, it is interactive and requires you to think, meditate, write, think strategically, and execute globally. We are in this together and this should be the first of many exercises to allow you to move forward and let your actions speak to the things you started out to do. This book is organized in the following manner to get you through this initial process. Each chapter is identified as a **Strategy,** serving as a tactical component to the overall plan to achieve in your personal, scholastic or business endeavor...**The Premise** lays the foundation for the strategy to give an understanding of its purpose and how it will affect your overall success...**The Rationale** gives justification and validation as to what makes this an important factor; it brings clarity, ensures proper guidance, and provides details in early stages of building or during the repairing process...**The Wall** gives an illustrative synopsis with a hint of a real-life perspective via my journey detailing how I prepared myself mentally, physically, and spiritually to achieve in instances of adversity and victory. Additionally, the Wall Coaches You through brainstorming, writing, planning, and executing that in which you were called to do in life. Despite the walls that may be around, you have the power within to overcome and do exceedingly well in all you set out to do. Therefore, NOW is the time to tap into YOUR VISION and take the steps to execute with every fiber in your body and this book is the first step to lay the foundation.

Introduction

Evicted to Build: My Life, My Passion...My Ministry

Blog Post: May 6, 2013... "So today has an emotional day and a reflective one. I started writing this post a week ago and many things have held it up, including my own apprehensions about the nature of the content. However, when I began to think of the source of my inspiration and motivation to move forward and excel in my entrepreneurial journey, it was only fitting that I stop and take a moment to briefly share my TESTimony. It may help some, others probably gone read and give a quick -_-, and then there are some...well actually none of that matters....it's my story so let me get to it." (PAUSE: *Sometimes we have to stop wondering about what others are going to think and feel about our life's journey...clear your mind and live life as God intended!)*

After building a solid five year career foundation working at Morehouse College, I was led to pursue my long awaited entrepreneurial endeavor...to own a conference and special events planning & design company. In 2009 that dream was realized with a trust fall on faith that led to the formation of The V2L Corporation, LLC (formerly V2L Events, LLC), a business services & management firm focused on developing, promoting, and protecting the client's brand image. By 2011 the demand shifted to branding & marketing and fostered the development of the V2L Design Studio. The founding vision and current practice is to make V2L a "one-stop" branding solutions firm to assist with event planning, branding, and marketing in one seamless production package. Additionally, my commitment to assisting others in business and entrepreneurial development led to creating The Entrepreneurial Cooperative (2012) and The 168 Life Project (2014). These aren't simply business endeavors to gain fame and wealth, yet they have become a manifestation of what I had to learn to be my passion and ministry. However, when I began to think of the source of my inspiration and motivation to move forward and excel in my entrepreneurial journey, it was only fitting that I stop and take a moment to briefly share my TESTimony. The next pages will not be a rags to riches story, but one of how my life transformed into a pursuit to assist others in reaching and obtaining their life-long goals and ambitions.

When I first decided to start my blog (The168Life.tumblr.com) the intent was to document my journey as an entrepreneur... including the trials and tribulations ... for those that think it's a simple and easy task. At no point did I think about making it a retrospective documentary to include how I became an entrepreneur. This was mainly because I didn't feel I was ready for the self-sufficient life of self employment and wanted to share from the perspective of someone that had a considerable amount of experience. In this time and space I have been assigned with the task to share my TESTimony to explain in more detail how this journey came about and its significance to those that have been destined to read this. Throughout my life, I have been the one that folks were quick to make assumptions and accusations about me for things totally unrelated to me. I had been deemed an only-child, nerd, selfish, from an affluent upbringing, arrogant, and the list goes on. Needless to say, most of this was brought on by me. Even when I was young I was well-mannered, neat, took extreme care of myself and belongings, treated folks with the utmost respect (until the crossed me the wrong way), and just simply carried an altruistic demeanor about myself and business in general. Therefore, I felt that my life was to only be shared with folks that were "significant"...this is actually still the case...meaning just a smile, handshake, and common courtesy exchange does not make us aspiring lifelong friends or short termed bff's (business friends forever).

In my maturation and growing, I now realize that my journey has become one that was meant for someone else, but I was entrusted with carrying the load. Trust me in 34+ years I have endured trials, tribulations, and tests that, when combined, would have probably wiped someone else out. I know because it almost did for me...but even in my lowest moments, which no one really knows about, I wasn't allowed to die nor deemed to give up. It always amazed me of how folks chose to be jealous towards me or anything I have accomplished. I work harder than the hardest working person I know and the difference is I don't go around broadcasting it...I just simply "Make IT Happen" by any means necessary. So to judge me and my journey without knowing my story, or anyone's, is a sad state of being. So 30 years in two sentences...I was born in the housing projects of

Savannah, GA, to a single parent mother that raised 5 kids and I managed to always do well in school despite my shyness and extreme introverted demeanor. In any attempt to fit in, I downplayed my intellect to become an "average" student, went to college, worked, obtained a master's, and started a business. Since the age of 15, I worked to gain the independence of acquiring things needed (not wanted). Never wanted to burden anyone so my take was to always work for everything, and ask ONLY when it's absolutely necessary...still practiced to this day. So did/do folks really see the hard working, diligent, tenacious, and persevering spirit inside? Rarely! Rather they see the spoiled side (although I have always worked and never had a problem getting support from those who nurtured and fueled my work ethic)...they see/saw me as mean (although I am well-known for motivating people to reach their fullest potential but only if they are willing to face their shortcomings because I challenge them in their thoughts to strive for better and stop thinking with such low aim)...they see/saw selfish & stingy (although I have given my last, whether I had it or not, to those I felt deserve it. All my blessings have been a revolving cycle because as I receive, somehow folks come into my life with a greater need and in obedience I share)...they see/saw me as lacking for nothing (although I have experienced job loss, a car repossession, apartment eviction, and only get money when I work on a client project...this is actually the summation of my entrepreneurial period 2009-present).

So my TESTimony is that I am a living example of what it means to not look like what you have been though. My journey was never defined by how I looked on the outside, although I was deteriorating on the inside. My battle with depression while in college is the reason I spent three extra years in pursuit of a BS in Mathematics...definitely not an easy task. The only folks that even knew of this "spirit of depression" was school counselors, which actually made it worse and led to an even deeper borderline suicidal mentality. Why?...because everyone thought they knew what a depressed person "looked" like. In those seven years, I had been robbed at gun point, experienced an apartment fire only to be moved and then burglarized, had a roommate that tried to take my life, was told that "I would never graduate with a math degree by a department "advisor", and experienced a series of health, mental, and financial issues that a person my age should not had had to deal with...But GOD. After graduation, with my math degree, things got worse before better.

Due to the suffrage of my g.p.a. finding a job was an entirely different journey despite the countless contacts in my direct network with recruiters, hiring managers, and other connects...there are some things that natural beings cannot help you out of. However, divine favor had a plan and I was GIVEN a temporary job as my bridge, but a shift in the atmosphere turned it into a professional career that many felt I was not qualified to do. Once again, I had to close my mouth and show my work ethic and decree that those folks could speak nothing over any part of my life. By this time I had entered the war zone with my adversaries unknowingly and some of the very people I trusted were the same ones in the midst of the most catastrophic period of my life...when I lost my job...shortly after not being able to deal with the pressures in one position so I decreased my salary by ($9k+) to take another position because I pursued happiness and my passion. But it's true when they say folks unhappy with themselves don't want to see others happy.

After the approach of a 5 year milestone, the time had come for that chapter to close. But like any good book or dramatic episode, it didn't end pretty and the transition should have been the end of the line. Just as I told my students and the hundreds I was able to speak life into as they came to the campus, the words of Dr. Benjamín Elijah Mays kept resonating in my spirit... **"In whatever you do, do it so well that no man living, no man dead, and no man yet to be born can do it any better."** So I took one month as I was trying to get my affairs in order to seek the face of God and figure out what I did to deserve the outcome...until I was reminded of "the" deal, which was that I was not to remain in my "temp" job past 5 years...I didn't factor in that the temp job could become permanent with benefits and a salary close to $40k (which was still low for the position). Nonetheless, that assignment was DONE and while in the valley I created my company and petitioned for grad school for the fall (at the end of recruitment season for any program). In this instant the game had totally changed. I went from being jobless to entrepreneurship, I got accepted into my master's program, and I was selected as a featured contestant on a new game show that has reached international airwaves...all within the first 6 months...the eye of the tornado.

As I bring this to a close...this transition tested every ounce of my faith and trust that God had a plan for my life as he revealed it will be used as an example to many that have dealt and/or dealing with what I have. In the midst of nearly completing my 2 years of graduate work my motivation for that field dwindled by more than 50% (still graduated with a 3.83 gpa). My 2009 Altima, which I financed BRAND NEW, was repossessed because I didn't have the capital to make the payments forcing me to reacquaint myself with MARTA (Atlanta's public transportation). My living situation became unstable as I exchanged roommates, struggled to maintain all my bills with an uncertain cash flow...was frozen out of one home and landed into a condo where I remained until 7 months after the completion of my master's...Only to end up on a sofa with my possessions in storage (which I still have). Last year I was blessed to regain independence with a new apartment and as the storm returned I was evicted only to be linked with a repurposed space that I called home. And yes I did just celebrate the 5 year anniversary of my company only for folks to still continue to ask me..."Have you found a job"..."Are you alright...how are you getting by"..."Do you think you should lower your standards until you get back stable"...and that list goes on. Whereas those folks never opened a pocket nor a door, but they are sooo friendly. -_-

This TESTimony, although previously written for blog purposes, was shared because I simply wanted to encourage YOU to NEVER give up on yourself. I don't care how hard it looks, how rough times get, or how low it may seem that you have fallen, YOU will never be given a challenge in this life that you are unable to conquer. My arrogance has not allowed me to focus on what others thought of me, even when it was tearing me down inside. So for those that think my entrepreneurial journey is a hobby, please understand it is a passion and labor of love that I genuinely care for and intercede in the business life of my clients. My credentials, experience, portfolio, and service delivery is my burden of proof of what I have done dating back to 1999, so not for one moment should anyone think that my business venture was simply a new thing or a side hustle for employment relief. The V2L Corporation will be known as the company that started from nothing and that carefully selected its clientele with the intent on delivering on its promise. I value everyone that give me the opportunity to assist in making their vision a reality whether it's a logo, business card, website, and for some their actual business. I do not take what I do lightly and I execute with a full boldness and expertise that the job will get done if I am allowed to do what I was hired to do. My days of micromanagement ended April 23, 2009 and my best executed projects have been those where I wasn't looked at as some business owner just starting out. V2L isn't for everyone and I accept that fact because we operate with integrity and high standards. Even in the midst of having unsettled debts that await the cash flow, I am honored to be around those that at some point in this journey have supported the vision, even if for a limited time. Regardless, the growth continues, everything owed WILL be paid, the services WILL continue to be strengthened, and our prayers WILL have everlasting effects, domestically and abroad.

So as I close, for real, note that your journey, whether as an entrepreneur or an employed lay person, isn't defined by your role, but by how you execute it. Think beyond your circumstances and environment and don't ever allow anyone to define you or put you in a box. So before you (not YOU, but the person on the side of you) decide to judge or be mad at what I have attained, what I do not have, or the "unfair advantage" you think I have, just reach deep inside and focus on you. I could have been much further than I am, but because I was afraid to go deep into the water, I allowed apprehension and fear to hold me back and I masked it by blaming it on the things and time spent doing for others. But know that no one is going to invest more into your vision than you are willing to put in.

Evicted to Build is a metaphor of how I had to not only die to myself, but had to be forced to separate from those people, places and things that were not needed for where I am destined to go. In that process comes the Building up of the new me which spreads the wealth by building up others. We are quick to try and hold on to things that do us more harm and have little desire to move out the comfort zone of complacency and content as a means to walk into our purpose. The more I prayed to God to allow me to follow HIS will for all that I was destined to do, the harder life seemed to get. The more I longed for material possessions, the more I began to lose, thereby making my hard work seem to be done in vain. But as I am reminded of the God I serve, the more I realized that my purpose and prosperity resided in my praise and thanksgiving for what I already have inside that needed to be shared with others. My faith grew stronger allowing me to better cope with living life on purpose and with purpose for the sake of saving someone else's.

I've got a TESTimony...

Let me introduce you to my Passion,

my Purpose, and

MY VISION!

Nicholas "Nick" Bartley, M.Ed

Strategy 1:
STOP, and go Pray...

Premise:

Despite your situation and as you desire to excel and achieve, seek inspiration and guidance through prayer & meditation to ensure you thoroughly know how to execute the Vision.

Rationale:

Vision and ideas do not simply POP into one's mind, it is something that was divinely implanted and just as a time capsule, it was due to be released at a specific point in time. Most people feel certain skills, training, and knowledge are needed and when those things have not been actualized at the time of the vision, they tend to push it off "until the time is right". That is fine, however, that is the time to find your mental space and go before the Creator and evoke knowledge and strength to understand more about the Vision and its purpose and at that time it will be revealed the direction you should go. Once you start operating in order, the pieces will fall into place, to include resources, people, and knowledge. Business endeavors that follow in line with a passion tend to be successful because we put additional time and effort to learn, practice, and execute since those activities create inner happiness. So the key is to not think that these ideas just randomly popped into your head and to take a moment to really think it through and use your prayer time to write the vision and everything else that has been given to you related to executing.

The Wall: TRUST & Believe...You were CHOSEN!

Matthew 6:33[1.1] - 1 Thessalonians 5: 16-18[1.2]...Amen

What started as a seemingly devastating situation nearly 5 years ago was actually a blessing in disguise. Didn't fight nor question it and glad I was obedient...leaned on faith, prayed and meditated on what to do, followed the necessary steps, and put in the WORK. When you ask God to enlarge your territory make sure you are ready for it and understand what it means... and it is not only about $. This happens when you're obsessed with your passion and trust God to do what he said and all that you have asked. Hear the call and move into your destiny. Now it's time to elevate and keep moving forward with no time to waste.

It's amazing how often we are ready to blame others for our misfortunes and circumstances, failing to realize that God is forever in control and have ordered our steps along the way. Yes we are to learn from the various experiences we endure, but most importantly we have to make sure we keep the open connection with the higher power that reminds us to seek Him daily for guidance and instructions. In my entrepreneurial journey, I had to re-learn how to trust and renew my faith. My tests and trials came in a manner that I did not think I had strength to deal with. It was a genuine encounter where those I put trust into turned out to really inflict more harm than to assist me in moving forward in achieving my life's dreams and goals. In what I deemed as a valley was meant for me to remove my faith and trust in man and get back at the feet of Jesus and seek guidance for my life. During that period I didn't have time to focus on what happened, the people involved, nor dwell on worrying about what was to happen next. The initial part of the test was over and it was time to apply what I had learned, been training for, and have used to assist others...now it was time to use it all for myself.

Know and understand that your faith and belief will guide you and send the correct people around at the times you will need them the most. Often times the assistance come from those you least expect, which is why it is important to love all and wish harm on none. Pray and meditate on your situation without involving others that cannot do anything for you. I spent a month semi-isolated before I knew that my next steps were to move towards my goals of entrepreneurship and graduate school. Two things I was terrified of, not sure why, but blessed enough to enter into with ease and self assured that I was going to be victorious and successful by any and all means. Without realizing it, I was careful not to let too many folks get in my ear and speak to my situation with their thoughts for my life and decisions. If you only grasp one concept out of what I am saying I want it to be this:

The folks you are around may be great company, but do not allow them to dictate your destiny. They come for different reasons and depending on how true you are to understanding and fulfilling your purpose and calling, those very folks could either elevate & push you to higher heights or they with will push you in the grave to kill the inner dream & visionary that resides within. I refused to allow myself to get stuck in a situation based on circumstances I could not control...but what I did know is that I could pray, shake it off, get myself together, and step into a new direction without a desire to look back. We live this life alone and there are times where we will outgrow those we hold near and dear, but understand that we all have the same opportunities to succeed and excel in any endeavor.

NO ONE can keep you from being great...

NO ONE can force you to make good/bad decisions...

NO ONE should have to pat you on the back every time you do what's RIGHT...

NO ONE should have to push or pull you to keep working hard and give it your best every time...

NO ONE should have to remind you to smile, keep joy within, and don't sweat the small stuff...

NO ONE, absolutely no one, except the Almighty and YOURSELF!

See when I was down and out, all my thoughts bounced off the walls and back to me. My isolation cave became my think-tank and I began to build billion dollar dreams and plans on how I was going to execute to cash in. I refused to sit and plot out shortcuts or quick schemes to get me by, yet I chose to build a legacy that would be a platform to show others how Awesome the God I serve is and that without Him I am nothing. Remember it all starts from within and everything we are to become and do in life has already been planted in us before we were created. Now it's time to move in your destiny and not because it will enhance your swag or become a trending topic, but because you know that there exists greatness within you and you know you do not have to settle or await validation from others. You are all you need and everyone else is only part of the supporting cast...they should know their role and play their position and nothing else.

I was CHOSEN for this...(repeat 3x)

So let's have a quick heart-to-heart and mind-to-mind on this. We are all placed in the world for a specific assignment and our works are designed to help someone else. At no point early in my business did I think I would be an "effective" top selling author and speaker {sometimes you have to speak into the atmosphere} that's a change agent advocating for people to not just be caught up in the moment, but to ensure their deeds build a legacy that keeps on giving.

So the thing we all know is that it is extremely difficult to think in chaos and operate in the midst of confusion and disorder. Now is the time for an internal assessment of what you really desire out of life. At no time do I tell people who to pray and meditate to because that is within your personal belief. What it does suggest is that you find that quiet time to seek clarity and guidance on you mission, goals, objectives, and the manner in which to execute them. At no time do I think people are given ideas that they cannot execute, it becomes a matter of how well they feel they can take on the challenge and move forward until the task is complete. So now let me just get right into this message.

My biggest gift has been to motivate people in ways to where they feel rejuvenated, excited, and ready to get in the game and win. Your life and ALL that has come with it has its place and purpose. Make it a point to repurpose those situations and extract the learning tools needed to unlock the next level of life. Every job you have, or will have, is designed to equip you with skills in people relations, fiscal responsibility, stress and anger management, conflict resolution, and other trade specific skills. Now to understand that your job should also make you happy, but the key is to work it, gain necessary knowledge, and keep it moving. Do not allow yourself to get complacent and content to the point where you're showing up and it simply becomes routine and your expectancy becomes a low aim. You were chosen because you possess skills and abilities others did not and where as your job searched ended, there's kept going. Think about being in school, the level doesn't matter, but imagine the aspects you disliked the most and the resistance you put up against it. The resistance came from the unwillingness to change your mind-set about what you did not know. No one likes to be challenged in any way that makes them uncomfortable and instead of embracing the changes that were divinely ordered, many simply repelled so they could still feel in control. One of the things we are rarely taught is that we should make choices based on how they would increase our marketability and value. You were chosen to be in those instances because it was designed to prepare you for something greater in life. While at this yield sign, make a slight turn to the right and think about those people you chose to associate vs. the ones that didn't make the cut. It is always great to be with like minded people, but were they selected based on how well they would support and push you toward reaching your dreams? Or was their selection based on a current status and association that you felt put you in a better position in the mind of others? Despite a person not making your team, how did you make them feel when you came in contact with them? I learned that it never hurt you to smile and say hello. Two simple gestures that do not obligate you to anything and they show you as a human being in support of mankind. People will always remember how you made them feel if they never remember anything else.

U-turn...apply the same thoughts to you. Think of the experiences that could have changed and challenged you for the better. Exchange your negative doubts for positive fuel to help you on your journey. Ensure that you always make yourself feel valued and selected because in your journey, you are really all you have in the main role. Your supporting cast will follow your lead. You are destined for greatness, but you first have to realize your passion and purpose is contained within your genetic DNA to succeed and achieve in all that you do. However, in order to do that you cannot allow what you do not know or what you have not experienced to prevent you from taking the next step. Even in our success we have those other bucket list items that we want to accomplish at some point in life. So get up and go do it! Stop wondering if you will be good enough, it really does not matter what the other folks will think, you will NOT fail, and you shall succeed. At the end of the day, you have to live with your conscience and face the fact of giving an excuse of why you did not accomplish that goal. When the creator decided on the time period of your existence, there was a Vision implanted in you that was not given to anyone else. Yes! A special assignment with your name on it, no instructions, but every time you think about it you get this feeling that overtakes you and you begin to journey to a place where you have a sense of purpose and importance; THAT Vision is what popped in your mind, but you may or may not feel some type of way about it because you are not sure if the timing was right to activate it.

As we prepare to move into the first interactive activity of this book, I want you to know that your Vision was not a mistake and it is attainable. Be ready to put in the work and move forward. I went into a period of isolation just so I could better understand my purpose and make up my mind that I was going to succeed even if I had to fight the battle alone. YOU were chosen for the assignment not your family and friends so make sure that you persevere and evoke that tenacious spirit that will not allow anything to get in your way. Start thinking about all the great people that gave up...correct, you don't even know who they are. You will never be released to abort the Vision and frankly you will have more and more things that will remind you of what you were supposed to be doing. Those reminders are not a slap in the face, they are your reality check that you CAN still do it and right now more than ever. Light a match to ignite that fire inside to release the passion and excitement of what is getting ready to happen for you. The fact that you are reading these words means you will no longer be deterred by anyone, including yourself, from walking in your purpose. You are a mighty warrior with a mantle of victory resting upon your shoulder. Today is your day to go back and get all that was promised to you and you shall be released to dream again and be successful in your journey. I pray for a mighty release of all things that have held you bound to this point. May grace and mercy not only follow you, but may they keep you and propel you to the next level. We cancel the attacks of the adversary and the spirit of fear for they shall have no place within you or in the minds and tongues of those around you. We speak prosperity in the journey, increase in knowledge, enlargement of your territory, peace during troubling times, boldness with each new step into unfamiliar land, and a divine hedge of protection for all those that are assigned to your Vision. We expect a divine manifestation that will execute the Vision with passion and purpose as it touches the lives of others and serve a greater purpose with global impacts. Amen!

Now let's take a moment to identify and develop the foundation to your next level in life.

Coach You...

1. Identify the best time(s) and place(s) where you can focus without distractions.

   _____
   _____
   _____

2. Write what you desire (life goal(s)) in the form of a prayer.

   _____
   _____
   _____
   _____

3. When did you first conceive the Vision to start a company/organization?

   _____
   _____
   _____

4. Would you provide the product/services if no pay were involved? What would motivate you to continue moving forward?

   _____
   _____
   _____

5. What is the company/organization idea?

   _____
   _____

6. How did you come up with the concept?

   _____
   _____
   _____

7. Who are the key contributors/supporters in your life?

   _____
   _____
   _____

8. Has others given you input that changes your vision in any way?

   _____

8.1.1.What was changed? _____

8.1.2.Do you agree with the change(s)? Why/Why not? _____

8.1.3.Does this change increase the opportunity to manifest the vision into reality? _____

9. Do you desire to execute this vision full-time? Why? _____

   9.1.1.What would make this a reality?_____

10. Who does this idea help and how?_____

11. Do you feel you were divinely appointed to carry-out this vision?

12. Is this idea more so for investment/financial purposes?

13. What would keep you from executing this vision?

Strategy 2:
Understand your Brand...

Premise:

Understand that You are YOUR "brand", forming an inseparable bond. Everything you aspire to do in life will orbit around the decisions you made yesterday and the choices for tomorrow. Safeguard your image so it brands you positively.

Rationale:

Ask a person what their brand is and often times or not they will proceed to show you their logo...and if they do not have a logo you will get an excuse and probably questioned if you know someone that do graphic design. Is this person you? Well it's is a good thing we are having this discussion. Simple response: your brand is what you do, how you do it, and how your interactions make the recipients feel. Every interaction, good or bad, has an effect on the brand, including those you put on your team, whom have now become an extension of your brand. Every time you engage someone, their mind is going to go back to some other interaction they have had with you and will weigh heavily how open and receptive they will be with this new discussion. So the key is to make sure your track record and tangible evidence doesn't contradict what you are about to embark on. Oh and the way the logo comes into play...let's just say it becomes the target that invokes that good, or not so good, feeling upon sight. It can be the most exquisite and divinely designed representation in the world, but the impression made by the product or service will ignite a conversation that will attract potential clients or create a repellent all because of how that other person felt. Let's not forget the exaggeration that usually occurs during story time...now imagine it being about your company or organization. How will your brand make people feel when they hear your name or see your logo? The two are inseparable so let's take this discussion further.

The Wall: Your work will Speak when your Mouth can't...

In the daily grind, hustle & flow, it is easy to fill the day with meaningless tasks and we end the day feeling empty because it seems none of the major obligations got done. That is often a result of being unfocused and we find ourselves completing our own level of "busy work". In understanding your Brand, you have to be able to understand who you are and what you're supposed to be doing. Maintaining self order and control can often be a difficult task, but not one that is impossible. For myself, I have always been in a level of high demand as people began to get to know me, my talents & skills, and in another life my ability to not understand the use of the word "NO". So my focus would often be thrown off because others had a plan for my life that was focused around their needs and I would often temporarily abort my mission to tend to their needs. Don't get me wrong, there is absolutely nothing wrong with helping others, but you must be able to identify and discern a distraction upon contact.

Sometimes you got to say, "**No distractions** formed against me **shall prosper!**

So what happens is you become consumed with the matters of others to the point to where you are left empty and too restless to deal with your own. Now how does this affect your brand? Understand that everything you do becomes evidence to support the perception and image to others.

May the work I DO speak for me...

To know me in a professional space means you know I have a special and intimate passion for branding and it is like tugging my heart when we enter into discussion on the topic. So I will warn you now that this coaching section is going to make you request a break before you get to your activity. It is best we get this out of the way early on in our cultivation process so that you can form an understanding of how you may be being perceived by others. This strategy is about knowing you. As you already know, branding in this context has minimal to do with logos and graphics and has everything to do with you and your subliminal messages to everything around you.

I entitled this section to represent the fact that your words mean very little if they contradict your actions. I have an awesome business associate that frequently speak about showing up and doing the work. As someone that is always working on self improvement and reaching to obtain the next level, I can tell you that I rarely speak on anything I have no experience with. When I am asked to do something I often refer to something that I have done or request testimonials that speak in my place. If I do not know something then I make it my business to seek knowledge and improve my skill set. So from this sentence forward, I need you to keep in mind that ALL of your actions create a compilation of descriptors, feelings, emotions, and reflections of your brand. Your brand is fully controlled by the perception of others and it becomes a permanent part of you until you show otherwise.

This is a reflective strategy so there isn't a whole lot of coaching someone can do to help you do YOU. Therefore, it is imperative that you take these words and your strategy activity to better understand your brand and know whether or not if there are some corrective actions needed. So there are a few things I need you to always keep in check, and this applies to all audiences reading these words. The follow tidbits are a few things to consider in understanding the images you are portraying to the world.

Social media is awesome, but make sure you keep your personal situations (drama) out of public view. People are more prone to support, hire, or endorse those that do not draw unnecessary negative attention. Remember this is a public broadcast and everything reflects those you are connected with also.

Train those around you on how to properly represent and present you to others. Many of the times folks will downplay your abilities and play you to the left simply because they don't know what all they don't know about you. If you ask someone for a **reference**, make sure you give a resume, listing of the various activities and achievements you have achieved. It's an injustice to not equip people with the tools they need and if in a crunch they will provide an ineffective and bland correspondence that will speak nothing of you in the way you would want it to. If you ask for a **client referral**, make sure you provide information on your target audience, the services/products you offer, and a pitch that this representative can give to others. If you have an

online profile, make sure it stays up to date with your current information and thorough enough to represent you well; while you are not online, it is still working on your behalf. A blank or incomplete profile is one that should never be seen by anyone...it serves no purpose. Your **printed collateral** should be aesthetically pleasing, but the importance is the content. Ensure the information is accurate, highlights key attributes, and gives all means for someone to connect with you. Nothing is worse than you having to hand write information that will at some point become illegible and a collateral scar.

Be careful of co-branding tactics that seem harmless but can have a detrimental effect on your advancement. **Email** addresses should always be professional. There is no need to utilize an address that makes someone feel uncomfortable or violated by typing it. Keep it simple and make sure it is easy to identify who it belongs to. If you own a business, make the investment to acquire your company's domain and obtain a professional email that brands only your company or organization. The convenience now will become a hesitation later. If you look amateur, you will be treated just as such. **Websites** are tricky. Many providers are creating user friendly templates...for FREE...but the frustration comes when non-tech savvy individuals try to play webmaster. Additionally, if the company insists that their company name is in your domain, then you have been cobranded and that is a **no-no** if you desire to be professionally independent and not some non-paid advertiser for these companies. At least make them pay for the publicity you are giving them. **Promotional collateral**...the rule is if it looks like a 3rd grader did it using clipart and random photos, then do not allow your logo to represent your brand until it meets your approval. Anything that bears your image, logo, or any other brand representative, should be requested to be approved by you prior to distribution of any means. You cannot demand it to be changed, but you can authorize or decline the use of your graphics on the item(s).

Coach You...

1. What is (or was) your definition of a Brand?

2. What does your brand portray to the people you serve?

2.1. Or, what are you known for?

_____
_____
_____

3. What distinguishes your company/organization from others similar to yours?

_____
_____
_____

4. How do you deliver your products/services to your clientele?

_____

5. How important is customer service?

_____
_____

6. Do you have a Logo or design concept? ___YES ___NO
   6.1. Explain the meaning behind your logo's design?

_____
_____
_____

   6.2. Is your logo easy to get confused with another company/organization? ___YES ___NO
7. In what instances and settings do you NOT represent your company/organization? How so?

_____
_____
_____
_____
_____

8. How often do you tell others about your Vision or company / organization? Has that been working for you? Can you improve?

_____
_____
_____
_____
_____
_____

9. What are 5 things you feel when you discuss your vision?

_____
_____
_____
_____

Strategy 3:
write, Write, WRITE...

Premise:

Write the VISION and create the game plan as it was divinely given to you. Release your mind clutter, organize, and be ready to move forward in order and excellence.

Rationale:

Our thoughts come and go, but it is not until we WRITE something that we can see and refer back to, that we take necessary actions toward making it happen. If the Vision you were given for your company/organization is to happen, then you must write until all your thoughts are out of your head. THEN you can take the time to make it sound pretty, organize, color code and anything else that makes you happy. The key is to not think that you can fully execute with all your thoughts and ideas only existing in your mind. If you are to garner support in any way, your stakeholders are going to want to see something tangible. This is usually why people get real excited when you tell them an idea, but the moment you ask for their support (mentally, physically, or financially) they smile and say "sure thing...let me know when you have it all together first and we will take it from there". Yes they believe in you, but your aim is to prove you are serious and have taken the time to properly think, effectively plan, and is ready to sustainably execute. The creation of a business plan is not some trick your adversaries (hater) put into place to be a tedious task to discourage you, it IS your roadmap to assist you in successfully executing the Vision with excellence. Your plan is what allows you to know what knowledge, skills, resources, etc that you lack and need to acquire. Proper Planning Prevents Poor Performance ... remember what we discussed about your brand... this is one of the ways to further strengthen your brand and/or to repair it. Write IT (the Vision), make IT Plain, and Execute IT with Authority.

The Wall: Write/Speak (IT) into the atmosphere...

For whatever reason, people can come up with the most awesome ideas, but when asked to see the written version or plan you would think they were asked for a social security number and bank card. I know you do not have that problem, which is why I was referring to the other people. So this is why writing is so important and I need to make sure we are seeing eye-to-eye on this. They say put your hopes and dreams in the atmosphere as a means to create positive energy as you strive for them. Well, that's all good and all, but that alone will not get you any results. The best advice I have ever given to any student, mentee, co-worker, client, and now you is to write down your thoughts...point, blank, period. Writing first gives a release in your mind from all the thoughts and other things you may be going through. So as we work on this professional development, reaching for that business you want to start, or any other goals you desire to attain, I need you to promise that you will write them in a special place so you can revisit later in an effort to create a strategy to put them to work.

The ultimate goal is for you to get that Vision down to a place where you can support it with some awesome goals, strategies, and measure to bring it to life and make it happen. Yes, writing does make it a little more real and it will cause you to be more accountable, hence, that is what makes this strategy so important. Go back and think of those great ideas you (had) and forgot them. Today that mind set, if it was a struggle for you, will change. All the information you have read to this point and in the upcoming chapters was written in more places I care to mention. It started out desiring to write a book, then it developed into my subject and content, and voila...the walls started talking. Well after all the headaches, and crying, and then the joy. But this isn't about me, back to you. Why is writing so important? First and foremost, you have to let yourself know that you are serious about achieving these goals and milestones. This isn't some New Year's resolution, which you never really see too many people writing those down, mainly because some do not want to be reminded of them. So we are going to get our mind geared up with writing for a purpose and the common mission of achieving them. No excuses!

Keep in mind that writing is fluid, which is why we have erasers, backspace, and strikethroughs. Make it a practice to first write down your thoughts. No pretty words and phrases...JUST WRITE. When your uninhibited self is free to release, you will be amazed at what you will accomplish in this step. To think that once you write something and unable to make changes and updates is to misunderstand the process. Think less of it being a chore and more as a personal board meeting and you have to play the roles of Chairperson and Secretary. Revisiting and reviewing your thoughts is when you can begin to make edits and get them close to where they are shareable. In similar fashion of keeping a journal or diary, make sure you keep going back and add additional notes, give yourself action items and task assignments to complete, and jot down other key measurable points that will push you to get to the next step. I am always amazed, yet baffled, by things I hear people declaring they do not like doing and then they stand strongly in not doing so. It is very hard to make money with a business idea if you cannot take a moment to articulate your point so that others can understand. Do not simply research and find what someone else did similar to you and think you can find a few words to change up and you will be as successful as they were. Create your document (THE Plan) to hold yourself accountable. Additionally, when the time comes to hire someone, to assist in making the vision a reality, you have something they can go by as a blueprint to prevent them from putting their "own" spin to it.

So now on to the editing and revising...please take a moment to let your eyes rest from writing and then go back and organize your thoughts so they make sense to **you**. Draft writing will not be clear to anyone else and if you present something to someone without cleaning it up, you have officially been deemed as ...well I won't dare call you lazy, but if you want to know my thoughts then there you have it. The fact you took time and resources to get this publication and we are having this discussion means that "it IS my business" and I want to make sure you do it right. Again, this book is about YOUR Vision and you must be passionate about everything you do for yourself if you truly want to gain support from others.

I think that is more than enough about writing and either it will get you pumped or it has put you in your feelings...so let's switch gears. Just as I have clients write and email me their thoughts, we are about to do the same. They way you write and talk is the almost similar to how people are going to comprehend what you are saying. In case you haven't realized, you have been asked to write throughout this entire reading process. Unless you read and said you will go back and write your answers in later, if I may please be excused in doing this...smh. If you are guilty and know what that mean, let's do better, everyone else, whether you know or not, please proceed.

So this session is about to take the game up a notch so feel free to get additional paper to complete this part. Don't shy away from this intervention; we are going on the verge of a breakthrough. ☺

Coach You...

1. In list form, write words that describe your company, organization, school/career/personal goals.

   _____
   _____
   _____
   _____
   _____
   _____
   _____

2. What is your Vision? Write it as comes to your mind...revise later.

   _____
   _____
   _____
   _____
   _____

3. What is needed to accomplish the goals?

   _____
   _____
   _____

4. How much time is needed to complete each of the goals starting today?

   _____
   _____

5. What financial resources are needed?

   _____
   _____
   _____

6. What non-financial resources are needed to be successful in your endeavor?

_____

_____

_____

_____

7. What educational goals do you desire to obtain in life?

_____

_____

8. What skills do you currently have that you feel you need or desire to improve upon?

_____

_____

_____

9. How often do you share your goals and aspirations with others?

_____

10. Are those whom you share with supportive of your goals?

_____

11. How does the achievement of your goals allow you to assist someone else?

_____

_____

_____

12. Do you feel you need to work for someone else to gain experience before you journey on your own business venture? Explain?

_____

_____

_____

_____

13. What is best location (geographically) for you to accomplish your goals? How did you come up with this? Do you plan to take action on it?

_____

_____

_____

_____

_____

Strategy 4:
Develop, Grow & Expand your Network...

Premise:

Network...with Everybody...your purpose is your ministry as long as you operate in the gift instilled in you.

Rationale:

It is great to have a close circle of friends to encourage, inspire, and support you in your endeavors. However, in order for you to grow you have to understand how to move and operate outside of the familiar territory. Staying within your circle means you are willing to develop within a cycle that will at some point become constant, which means the growth, development, expansion, etc will become stagnate and eventually come to a complete STOP. As you seek to gain understanding of your purpose in life, how to effectively implement and execute the VISION, how to follow your passion without bringing on unnecessary stress, then it means you need to mentally be prepared to get out there and meet the world. They do not bite! Walking in your purpose is having an understanding that the people you are to have a positive effect on are those you have yet to meet. The connect that you need to get into school, get a job, advance in your career, or even expand your business maybe connected to those people you shy away from when your inner circle invited you to that event. Can you explain and sell yourself well enough to have others to become engaged and engrossed to what you are saying or doing to the point they are willing to go tell others of your awesomeness? Or are you going to listen to mainstream radio and social media and adopt the concept of "NO new friends". Get it in your spirit that the world is bigger than you and your circle and that it is designed for you to make a point to not miss an opportunity to connect with others and you will give them the chance to be blessed by knowing the gifts that were instilled in you. Keep a global perspective and be open to get out of your comfort zone as to not miss out on all that is in store for you and those around you.

The Wall: The Vision is bigger than that box...

It is great to know your Vision for **your** life, have attainable goals, and BIG Dreams, but are they designed to push you to the next level or are they set to a where you will be comfortable with easy and low results? The thing most of my mentees probably didn't like the most is that is seemed that I was rarely happy with their successes on achievements that were "good"...not to be confused with those that could be "Great". However, I was ecstatic, I was just displeased with the fact of when they settled and could have performed much better as I know they could. If you know you can achieve an "A" as long as you are focused, put in a little extra time, and give it your all, then why be happy when you simply get a "B" that you barely earned. The same is with life and pursuing those things you have a passion and desire for. Regardless of what's really required to obtain it, make up in your mind that you will always put in extra effort as a mean of self satisfaction. We often feel some type of way when we get things and have the feeling we didn't earn them. No matter what it is, there is a different feeling knowing that you stepped up to the challenge, conquered, and no one can refute the fact that you earned it. So when you strive to execute the game plan to reach all the goals you set out to do, the same philosophy goes and you have to make it a consistent practice to perform better than your normal or what is required. That is development and it means your mentality is changing about how you desire to go about routine matters and raising the expectations of what you will allow others to expect or demand of you. It is impossible for others to promote you as the best if they think or know you are a subpar performer and that it always takes extra motivation to get you to that excellent status. Your brand should dictate the contrary, that you always perform top of your game in every instance no matter what it is. This is what will cause folks to speak highly of you in times when you don't eve request them to. Your work ethic should exude a level of excellence that brings opportunities to you in abundance because you have a track record that is consistent and the outcome is commendable. A few off days are to be expected, but should never be the norm to where a great day surprises people. You have the power to change the perception you give off with time, extra effort, and hard work...consistently.

Now that the development of the foundation is in the works, let's begin to think about your growth. The body naturally grows daily, your mind yearns to learn new things, and your atmosphere should shift to the point where your "future you" is completely different than the current and past you. **To be taken serious in any endeavor, one must exhibit a level of growth and maturity that commands the respect it is due.** As the scripture tells us: "When I was a child, I spoke as a child, I understood as a child, I thought as a child: but when I became a man, I put away childish things (I Corinthians 13:11 KJV)[4]". Thereby meaning, when you understand where you want and desire to grow{go} in life, you have to make efforts to change into your desire. Seek understanding, increase your knowledge, and make sure you are effectively meeting people and accepting opportunities that will get you closer to that desire. Now is your time to walk with the other lions going in the direction you are heading, instead of staying in the fields with your bags packed ready to go, yet you remain still. Growth is an uncomfortable feeling because it throws in our face what we don't know. So I am here to tell you that from this page forward there is no longer a stranger you have never met, an opportunity you have never taken, nor a new skill you don't know. Accept the challenge and move into your destiny. The world is so much bigger than where you currently reside, so you have to take a flight and explore to find your niche and purpose.

The last key to this strategy is about expanding your network. This is a limitless conversation so if you are thinking network as people, then I need you to take note that this is NOT the case today. Your network for this purpose is going to work like the noun it is...people, places, and things that have been pre-assigned to your destiny to assist in your advancement. This includes family, friends, colleagues, and strangers that have a strong influence to connect you with more of the right people; it includes your hometown, other major cities, small villages, travel abroad where opportunities exist; and it includes education, learning new skills, humility to serve and bold enough to lead, and never being to prideful to execute tasks you are "over qualified" to do. See the way your network is set-up, your worth is dependent upon your work ethic and dependability and that is what will carry you to the next level on the strength and actions of those around you. There is nothing like getting an awesome and genuine recommendation from someone without you having to write it yourself and they sign. Exercising the option to expand this network is what will release your Vision to the world because they will be open and receptive to hear what you have to say and support you because you have put in the work. The time will come when your current position is going to change and shift and the comfort you once knew will make you anxious and squeamish. This is your time to explore and discover what else awaits you. Your decision to ride that feeling out is a sign that you are complacent in the situation and not interested in expanding...well "not right now" at least...right? Go into every situation with an exit strategy so you can get the most out of the "right now" in preparation for the future. No more complaining, drama, gossiping, dreadful days, blank stares, or just being negative period. Remember you chose your current situation and someone took a chance on you. So that same excitement you have when you started the journey, should be the current feeling while you are going through it, and should be heightened as you thankfully exit to take on the next assignment. You should never feel like you are in a "stuck" position; stuck is when you cannot shift into the next gear. Right now you are not only shifting to the next gear, but you are moving into a position that will be a set-up for you bloodline, you shall break generational curses, and continue to be the example of what it means to walk into your destiny with purpose. If you sat still and prayed after chapter 1 then by now you should be leaping for joy because your new day is waiting on you and we already know nothing is going to stop you. Point. Blank. Period. ... so now let's get ready to develop, grow, and expand the Vision.

Now that you are out of the box and have taken the limits off of your life and aspirations, let's take a moment to think critically on how to make this moment count. This is not the time to wait on someone to "put you on", you have to seize the opportunities that come to you in whatever form, and create the ones that are still outstanding. Sometimes expansion comes out of you birthing the opportunities needed so you can help someone else.

Coach You...

1. List 5 opportunities you are currently striving for right now, even if you haven't put any action towards it in a while.

_____
_____
_____

2. How often do you make a point to meet new people? Why or Why Not? What is your biggest obstacle when meeting people?

_____

_____

_____

_____

3. What is your current practice to follow-up with new people you meet?

_____

_____

_____

4. What skills, unrelated to what you do, would you not mind learning?

_____

_____

_____

_____

5. How would these skills enhance you personally and/or professionally?

_____

_____

_____

_____

The world is watching and waiting...on YOU!

Strategy 5:
Be Professional in all you do...

Premise:

Project a professional image at all times so that it reflects a positive perception, personally & professionally, to prospective stakeholders while also allowing those you know to understand your level of seriousness.

Rationale:

Very simple...DO worry about what others think. Well don't "worry" about anything, rather take these thoughts into consideration and develop a game plan to correct those areas that are in need. Often people want to operate in the "keep it real" mentality without understanding what it really means. Your self-assessment should include gaining an understanding of how people truly feel about you, whether it's through personal relationships with family or friends or professional opinions offered by co-workers and business associates. The key perspective is to realize that your aura gives off an energy that may be attractive or repulsive in the eyes of others and becomes the determining factor of their role as your advocate.

As people begin to support and endorse you and your endeavors, you now become a reflection of them and if they are even remotely apprehensive about you, your abilities, your attitude, and your future direction, then that is something you really need to know. Put it this way, how often do you promote businesses that seem to operate as a random thought or fly by night idea that is here today, but seem as if it is going to be gone tomorrow? Do not give others the ability to second guess your business venture. Legalize your business, commission professional representatives (website, business cards, logo, etc), separate your social media presence (personal vs professional), learn proper uses of social media, and stay current on marketing and promotional trends. Don't have a business you say?...well imagine you pumping up and speaking highly of your friend and they come around and totally contradict what you just said. This not only makes you look bad, but it causes others to question your judgment and integrity. Now imagine either of these scenarios being YOU. What can others say about you, your business...can they articulate your VISION and goals? Why or Why NOT?

***** ***** *****

The Wall: The smile, the tone, and the bow-tie...

Yes Sir, No Ma'am, Please, and Thank You will never go out of style and has no respective age of use. As the ultimate sign of respect, these gestures alone can take you places beyond your wildest imagination.

Your professionalism stems from your manners, whether inherited, taught, or learned, you must know how to treat others in a way that makes you pleasant to be around. As stated time and time again, people may not remember or care about anything you do, but the way you treat them will be remembered forever. So in the business of life, make sure your professionalism is genuine and comes from a place deep within so that it can assist in your advancement. Often times we humans get hotheaded at things we cannot control, especially if the outcome is not what we want. This is the most extreme waste of energy because it does nothing for you. I am often told I have a nonchalant demeanor and some folks are bothered by that...the fact that I do not negatively react to the situations that arise. Being level headed, respectful, and professional allowed for people to go out of their way to assist me in times and situations that they didn't have to. Additionally, I have had situations where I had to respectfully put people in their place, but because I was polite in my greeting and pleasant in my closing, I am not sure if they knew the news received was bad upon delivery. I am not a sugarcoat type person so I had to learn how to appropriately deliver news that will effectively convey the message. It is never what you say; it is how you say it.

Think about how you feel when you tell someone off then you turn around and have to ask them for something. Common courtesy is one of those things that honestly should not have to be a strategy in this book, but trust me, I have seen them range from rugged to polished and lack the simplest of manners. So this strategy will not ask questions, it will simply state some points in areas of professionalism that should be followed, maintained, or quickly mediated so that your move to fulfilling your Vision aren't tainted by the small things.

Manners & Courtesy...

Always greet others when you enter into a room or make eye contact in passing (even if you look at someone by mistake).

Say "Please" when you ask and "Thank You" after you receive. This could in turn assist in future assistance,

DO NOT assume, simply ask...yes it is that simple. Regardless of how much you like the response, if you had to ask, then it means someone else is in control and have the ability to change an outcome in your favor. So your actions will determine their reaction.

Social Media presence...

Online interactions are to be treated as entertainment ONLY. If you don't want people to discuss or misinterpret what you say, then either "think before you type" or "keep it to yourself". Virtual retractions are pointless.

If you have a professional brand you want to portray, make sure you separate it from your personal engagement if you decide to carry yourself in virtual life that contradicts/defames your character or tarnishes your image.

You are in full control of what you put out, but not in how others perceive you so do not give them anything to cause an unfavorable response to your presence.

Appearance & Attire...

Create your personal dress code to set a standard that represents you in various scenarios.

Your appearance either attracts or repels so it is important to make sure it's always clean, neat, appropriate, and that clothing is the correct size.

Be unique, but make sure you keep your audience in mind.

Your appearance WILL send a message and set a tone for any possible business transactions and/or should be relatable to your discussion.

Communication Etiquette...

Communications, regardless on the medium used, should always be clear understandable, and ensures that everyone involved effectively receives the message

Remember to set and let it be known your preference so others know how to properly communicate information to you.

Create communication hours where you tend to be more available.

Have response periods that are sensible and have a risk management plan if you happen to respond outside that timeframe.

If certain deliverables are required to be met before a response is to be given, then make sure the receiver knows that or simply provide a quick update to speak to the current status.

Work/Job Responsibilities...

Always be ON. You have plenty time to be off when you take vacations and naps.

Always execute to the fullest.

Give it your ALL or get out of the way. You should never be part of a company's customer service problem...even if its your own.

Say NO to excuses and YES to delivering what you promised.

Strive to Master the small things, conquer the harder tasks, and accept the challenge of tasks that are new. It's called Growth.

Make politeness & courteousness permanent.

Leave personal issues at home or in the car.

Recommendation/Referral requests & Follow-ups...

Always request recommendations/referrals in writing and provide ALL pertinent information that will be needed to all for an appropriate response and effective delivery of the request. Nothing is worse than being asked to do something to benefit the requestor, but they fail to provide the needed information.

Be sure to offer an appropriate "Thank You" to all whom you correspond with for these requests regardless of their decision to assist or not.

In your initial request, feel free to request a time to talk to provide additional information. DO NOT put people on the spot with random calls or asking them in passing.

Strategy 6:
Build your "A" Team...

Premise:

Choose your circle to be those moving in a positive direction...ordain your team according to where they are most beneficial and effective...Many may call, but few should be chosen, so choose wisely.

Rationale:

Personally speaking... Your immediate circle, which often includes family, friends, and even some stalkers, should be close guarded to the point to where they become your biggest cheerleaders and supporters. When you are around them it should be a joyous occasion of fun, laughter, chastising even, and offering constructive critiques that will assist you in furthering yourself to the next level. Now if this circle includes folks that feel they need to put you down, as a means to build you up, to the point to where it becomes demeaning and belittling, then you need reevaluate that...well we will call it a "relationship" for the sake of discussion, mainly because that person just may happen to be family. Do not contaminate your pursuit of greatness by valuing opinions of those too afraid to love and motivate themselves. Instead, assess what they are doing with their lives and validate their respective role in your life. You are in control of your personal "Board of Directors" to guide you through your journey.

In the name of business... When conducting business, your Team directly affects your bottom line. As a new business owner, most people look at this as the perfect opportunity to assist you and invite themselves to your team, or they anxiously accept your invitation because you know they will accept whatever you are able to pay them, which is fine as long as they are qualified or trainable in a manner that best represent your brand. Building the "A" Team means acquiring individuals that can understand, enhance, and support the VISION without compromising its mission and purpose for self gain. To utilize people as a matter of convenience means you are willing to risk all that your business is and can be for the sake taking a shortcut that will cost you in the long run. There is a difference in your operational team and your support team...make sure everyone know their role and play their position.

***** ***** *****

The Wall: My Team is A-1 and they chose ME

Everyone thinks they have a dynamic team, until times get rough and their actions prove otherwise. Has this ever happened to you...when you needed that ride, wanted to hang out, asked for an honest opinion, needed a hand setting-up, or whatever the situation may have been? The real question is, did you choose the team, were they already given to you or did they choose you? We all should have our own personal board of directors, people we can count on, trust, value their opinion, and who will give it to us straight with no chaser. It is great to be selective and fill the various roles with people that qualify and fit, but make sure they are also vested in the process. They need to be as excited, if not more, to be able to fulfill such an honor. However, you in turn should make sure you show your appreciation if you desire them to be dedicated and loyal to your Vision. Remember that your vision means a hill of beans to their own personal vision so the least you can do is not treat them as an extra that you promote and demote at your leisure. No one wants to be taken for granted and this is the time to take a deep assessment at how you value your personal, professional, and business relationships and the people directly connected to you.

Your team is more dynamic than you think. Every time you need someone else in order to complete a task, guess what, they are on your team. How you make them feel is what determines if their membership becomes an asset or liability. So before we start analyzing whether or not if you have the "A" Team or not, here are a few nuggets to keep in mind before assigning positions or giving pink slips.

The strategy of Building your Team:
❖ Know what you need and interview everyone. No matter how well you think you know what they can/cannot do.

❖ Do not settle for a warm body and cute smile. Qualify their actual skills and abilities in relation to how they can meet your needs.

❖ Be knowledgeable in all things you assign to others. Do not play yourself and be naïve with bringing an "expert" on the team. Just because you don't want to do it doesn't mean you don't need to know how.

❖ Don't just do what you are told, do what needs to be done...should be the adopted way of thinking. Everyone should have a self starter attitude and be ready to work for the Vision and not just their personal gain.

❖ Make sure there is a personal and connecting motivation that will allow team members to take charge in seeing the Vision executed to completion. Being personally invested in a project, while knowing that its success will propel them in some areas, is always a good motivator to get the best work ethic and operational excellence in the execution of their assigned role.

❖ Keep the focus on working as a Team, not individual agendas.

❖ Treat everyone with respect in public and private settings.

❖ Value their time and trust their level of expertise...otherwise don't bring them on. No one wants to be expected to work and operate in excellence if not given the opportunity to do such. No one wants to be micro managed,

So as those points marinate, let's really understand your thought processes in team building.

1. With understanding your present Vision and Goals, what type of team do you need? Friends, staff, business partners, etc...identity what you need to be successful.

_____
_____
_____
_____
_____
_____
_____

2. Why are these people needed?

_____
_____
_____

_____

_____

3. How do/will you show your appreciation?

_____

_____

_____

_____

4. What are the top 10 qualities you need in building your "A" Team?

_____

_____

_____

5. What additional personal development will be needed to keep your team on top of their A game? Or do you not have any interest in them staying on point with their skills and abilities? (take your time with this one)

_____

_____

_____

_____

_____

_____

_____

_____

_____

_____

_____

_____

_____

_____

_____

_____

_____

_____

Strategy 7:
Relationships...

Premise:

Maintain professional relationships at all times...consistency is key in acquiring and retaining healthy relationships with friends, clients, vendors, and industry colleagues.

Rationale:

Value the right people for the right reason and don't let them beat up your WALLS. Now we are all grown and know the various connotations that can be taken in and they ALL apply. When you exchange contact information, dialogue, and pleasantries you know exactly your intentions and so does the other party. So to keep it professionally candid...don't use what you got to get what you want. Retaining and maintaining healthy relationships is hard work and you must understand that it requires constant work. It is impossible to always feel you can neglect a personal or business connect and just simply pick it back up when you need something. Keep the lines of communication open and know what the purpose you have for interacting and what's expected in return. Do not start any habits or make any promises you are not willing to keep. Your word and follow-thru is what solidifies a relationship as time progresses and it has to become fully developed. No mother would dare rush a pregnancy knowing that the baby still has some development to do within a safeguarded environment. Same premise. Put in the work to show yourself approved to EARN the friendship of a friend, client, business partner and whomever else. Make it a point to really get to know them as it helps to foster conversation and interaction that will be genuine. Serious people have no time for idle conversation and do not desire to sow seeds in infertile grounds. In 2006, I learned through experience the meaning and essence of the word "altruism", the unselfish concern for others. Show people that you care and you will build a relationship that will foster other relationships and those needs and desires you have will start to materialize naturally. People will begin to bless you in ways you cannot imagine because they will see and know your needs without you constantly reminding them. So know and understand that you never really know how and why you need someone, but the way you make them feel will determine what they are willing to do, why, and what they want in return.

***** ***** *****

The Wall: Know when to hold 'em, fold 'em, or walk away...

If you don't have any other great takeaways from this section, just know that not all relationships are healthy and needed in order for you to succeed. You have the power and ability to know and discern when those around you mean you no good. The great Kenny Rogers sang it best:

"You've got to know when to hold 'em, know when to fold 'em,

Know when to walk away, know when to run. You never count your money when you're sittin' at the table, There'll be time enough for countin' when the dealin's done."[7]

Just as misery loves company, successful folks only strive to be around other positive, successful, forward thinking, goal oriented, and successful people. Yes I was feeling some type of way writing that. You cannot go through life thinking that everyone that appear to have it going on need to be part of your circle. When you develop top quality relationships for purposes of friendship, business, romantic, or any combination, you have to make sure that you are digging deep an understanding what resides within that hasn't been released to the "new" public. Candidly, make sure you know what the streets know. The moment you get that feeling in your gut that something isn't quite right about the situation then, refer to Strategy 1, consider Strategy 2, execute Strategy 5, and take the necessary actions as the situation dictates. Just as I have been asking you questions throughout this entire reading, be ready to interview people, and businesses, before you decide to connect. Ask the questions without hesitation. It isn't being nosey as long as you keep the focus on those things that validates work ethic, integrity, and their intentions and expectations. This will then allow you to know which action from the song that you need to listen to...and if it's "Run" don't procrastinate by doing a slow walk...Keep IT Moving!

So now, let's do a QUICK assessment of your relationships past, present, and future. This is designed to take into account your professional and business associations. Family you are stuck with, and if you can apply to other interactions, then by all means make some moves.

1. How well can you depend on your valued relationships in time of need?

_____

_____

2. Has there ever existed moments where your associates could have assisted you in a situation, without jeopardizing themselves, and they did not do so? Explain.

_____

_____

_____

3. Whom have you been able to count on without the need to feel lesser of yourself in your moments of need?

_____

_____

_____

4. Flipping the script, what situations existed where you could have helped someone without causing a strain on you? (Apply to all situations: giving to homeless, giving an "offering" to a friend, referring someone for a position/gig they were qualified to execute, etc...)

_____

_____

_____

_____

_____

5. What steps do you take to get to know new connections?

_____

_____

_____

_____

_____

6. Do you determine and categorize your relationships based off of what you are able to get out of the relationship?

_____

_____

_____

_____

_____

_____

7. Do you get in your feelings when you feel people do not support you the way YOU want them to? Do you ask why? Can you accept and respect their decision? Why or why not?

_____

_____

_____

_____

_____

_____

_____

_____

_____

_____

_____

_____

_____

Strategy 8:
Execute with Authority...

Premise:

Operate in your calling, execute with passion, know the game and play your role, and don't waste anyone's time.

Rationale:

If I haven't learned anything else from my experiences from high school to now, I learned that when put in a position of leadership or authority you surely must be ready to play the role. Not to the point where you wear arrogance and pride, but show humility with an iron fist. It is possible to lead while not seeking the spotlight. You can direct without degrading others. You can, and should want to, train and develop others to the point they know just as much as you...or more. Remember, when in an authoritative position, these people become part of your circle and they reflect YOU! If you improperly train someone then know it will come back on you and can very well cause you to lose respect. So the key to this strategy is to make sure you operate in what you have been called to do. If someone sees potential in you then make sure you take the time to expand you knowledge and grow in it. Chasing money does not equate to having passion, it simply means you can easily be bought and folks will have no problem throwing money in your face to control your every move. Take the time to learn your craft, have compassion for those under your tutelage, show up, and do the work. Some of the best leaders are those whose presence commands a world of respect. When you step into a room, OWN IT without boasting or bragging, but let your pleasant energy, charismatic charm, and fervor to be open and receptive to others by making them feel you appreciate the opportunity to get to meet them. When given the opportunity to gain a moment of anyone's time, make sure you cherish it and not waste it. Know how to make an impression without seeming thirsty, desperate, and passive, yet build a mutual desire to build a strong relationship and exude the confidence that was instilled in you since the very conception of your being. Walk into your destiny as a warrior ready to conquer the battle and know that you were created for this time & assignment and your talents, abilities, and gifts have made room for you to be openly received by others for the purpose of moving YOUR vision forward. Now execute with passion & purpose.

✳✳✳✳✳   ✳✳✳✳✳   ✳✳✳✳✳

The Wall: Passiveness doesn't pay the bills...

As you have reached the end of this book, I know you have been taken on an emotional rollercoaster, but in it all, I want you to know that your path and journey was created especially for you. Now is the time for you to make the decision that you will not allow anything to deter you, get you off track, or take you backwards. The mission of this book was to wake up the inner you that desires to explore new things, live without regrets, appreciates everything and takes nothing for granted, and above all maintains control of your life. Your time, efforts, and energy should not be easily effected by the actions of others...those are your emotions taking control. So know when to put the emotions in check, get out of your feelings, and DO NOT allow them to stop you from reaching your goals, making your money, taking care of your obligations, and being happy.

I will not make you complete any questions but I want you to read this affirmation and let it get in your spirit and make up your mind to rediscover those things that you feel you have lost control over. So whether you intended to go back to school, change careers, start a business, or to just be a better than the yesterday you, just know that NOTHING can stop that at all.

Your affirmation...
✓ I was created with a purpose;
✓ I have what it takes to accomplish my goals and achieve my dreams;
✓ I will not allow what I do not know (yet) to conquer my future endeavors without a fight;

- ✓ I am ready to step out of my comfort zone and explore new possibilities;
- ✓ I will DREAM BIG, push beyond the limit, and keep going until the goal is ACHIEVED!
- ✓ I will endure the pain to reach my purpose;
- ✓ I will conquer the unknown to pursue my passion;
- ✓ I will overcome adversity to show others it can be done;
- ✓ This IS my season and I was CHOSEN for this and now I will execute until my assignment is complete.
- ✓ My name is _____ and I AM a manifestation of greatness and today I will boldly walk into my destiny and nothing is going to stop me!

The key to executing with authority is changing your internal switch to believe you can do ALL that you set out to do. Our biggest hindrance prior to now was the desire to please others and putting their desires before our needs. Now is the time to think **TEAM ME** and go back and get your stuff. Reflect of what you hope to desire in life and what could potentially keep you from reaching it...now make your game plan to not allow those obstacles to be successful in their mission. The strategy to mastering the game of life is knowing how to outsmart, outthink, and outperform...yourself. Yes! You know yourself better than anyone else does and once you learn and realize that, all the decisions you make were made with some intent that you knew what the potential outcomes were going to be. So I challenge you to remove the external forces you thought influenced you, when you chose them. It's about accountability and not wanting someone else to hold you more accountable than you are willing to do for yourself. Why?...because that now gives them control of YOUR destiny. The happiest times in our life were those when we didn't know what we couldn't do, because we did it anyways; no thoughts on where we couldn't go, we just went; no limits or preconceived thoughts on what we didn't like, we just experienced it for ourselves and made our own decision. That should continue to be the focus as we press forward to go back and accomplish those old ambitions, goals, dreams and thank God for the chance to do so.

Who gon' stop you? Right, NOBODY, so go on ahead and read the Conclusion and get ready for a New Beginning. Even the most successful people have things they still hope to accomplish. I want to hear about your new adventures, aspirations, and new levels of happiness so don't just think of me as your paperback "homie" and hit me up. Think this way, *if you could not do it, then you would not have been able to think it!* You are your BOSS and you are in control!

Conclusion

It Could Have Been Me, BUT...

As I was pondering how to end this prolific illustration of my entrepreneurial journey and written coaching, I felt it had to be something profound that makes you go "hmmmm". Well, unfortunately that isn't going to be the case here. One day I was in the midst of assisting one of my residents, whom happen to be 60+ years old, with his resume. It was during this momentous exchange, given at that point we hadn't really experienced that bonding connection yet, that my spirit was implanted with a foreshadow of how my life could have turned at any of the instances I experienced that were all time lows for me. However, upon discovering a few commonalities, I began seeing somewhat of an older version of myself. More so, it hit me that my role at that moment could have been reversed and instead of serving these men, **it could have been me** receiving the same services. I won't go into any extreme detail and hopefully you have or will experience the live event to understand how this connects. So in a better context I want to assist in pushing your mental capacity to understand that in every situation there is another option that could have been chosen for your life. As you were prepared and shipped off to enter the world, your being was designed to make an indelible mark with a purpose that was specially encoded with an assignment that only YOU can execute. My job is to ensure you tap into that potential and to hold you to some level of accountability to ensure the mission IS NOT aborted. My life has been filled with obstacles, adversities, and experiences that I felt didn't belong to me only to later understand that my endurance allowed me to connect with almost anyone I encounter. Although I didn't understand it then, I have come to grips with understanding the reverse consequences that could have followed. Perseverance, tenacity, altruism, humility, obedience, and the list goes on, are not words for SAT prep nor multi-syllable words of proliferation to sound educated...they became my being, my purpose, MY LIFE.

So now we stand (sit, lay, etc) as you read these words, ready to embark on the next phase of this journey and move forward. No time to look back. We know some of those situations and scenarios you encounter or pass by daily could have been you on the other side, but you were chosen for a different purpose and on this day I decree

& declare that you shall walk into your destiny with a fire that keeps you moving forward. I speak an abundance of resources to come your way to make the load not lighter, but strength to endure to the end. We must encounter some things to show ourselves approved to be able to handle all that is to come our way. Whether you are to open a business, prepare for a promotion, fulfill those lifelong goals you set, position yourself for wealth accumulation, or to simply move in the path ordained for you through service, you have to ensure your mental state is ready and fired up to go. The journey of life is about strategy, execution, and completion. Once you start an endeavor you should also have the mindset of doing whatever necessary to complete it and not allow life's little distractions to get you off course. Accept the challenges and conquer them. Avoidance is like patching a cracked foundation with school glue...it just simply will not work.

The strategies you just went through are just the foundation to give you a starting place. Your next steps should be towards capturing all the thoughts that entered your mind as you were reading and organizing them into strategic and attainable goals. Not a New Year's resolution, bucket list, or simple "wishes", make sure this action plan infuses your passions, happiness, prosperity, and means to pay it forward. We always think we know how our lives could have ended up and become thankful, but do we ever realize that each day is a manifestation of a greater plan that was predestined? My challenge to you is to grab a hold of your vision and vow to not let it go until you fully experience life and all its challenges. Recognize your shortfalls and create a plan that will incorporate all the lessons learned into a strategy that can be applicable in a multitude of situations. Given you have reached the conclusion of this edition, you now should understand that our mode of thinking is to no longer dwell on the negative situations, but to find positive solutions. No more planning and putting out distress signals for a pity party yet celebrating each milestone as it comes. No longer chase after dead situations, yet find fertile grounds to sow into and pay it forward. If ever you need a reminder as to why you are giving more than you are receiving then it is at that moment only that you can take a look back. You purposely do not have eyes in the back of your head and in similar fashion your VISION should move you FORWARD only.

Now you are equipped with a foundation to get you started on the right track to strategizing and executing your vision. I quite possibly could have tried to put all the answers in this book, but then that would have been a smart business move on my part. LOL! Seriously, the issue comes from individuals wanting to read everyone else's solution for a problem instead of putting in their own work so I didn't want any reader to fall victim to that ideology. We are moving you into the mode of self-sustainable thinking to properly outline your personal strategic plan to get you to the next level. It has been awesome walking with you on this journey and I pray for your success in whatever your next endeavor finds you. Remember to act and walk like a BOSS because you got this and you are worthy and capable of making a positive change for you, your family, and the world around you.

You will not only succeed, but you will surpass your wildest dreams. Now close this book, take a deep breath, and **GO MAKE IT HAPPEN.**

Next up... Spring 2016! The remix designed specifically for High School and College students. Just in time for graduation season!

Pre-Order your copy today www.The168Life.com

Inspirational Text & References

The following are selected verses that correspond to each strategy. These texts stand as biblical principles, examples, and teachings that were used to create the foundation in which each strategy became relevant and substantiated. Read and Study them to gain your own understanding as to how you are to use in your own endeavor.

1) STOP, and go Pray

Matthew 6:9-13 KJV :: After this manner therefore pray ye: Our Father which art in heaven, Hallowed be thy name. Thy kingdom come. Thy will be done in earth, as it is in heaven. Give us this day our daily bread. And forgive us our debts, as we forgive our debtors. And lead us not into temptation, but deliver us from evil: For thine is the kingdom, and the power, and the glory, forever. Amen.

Hebrews 11:1 KJV :: Now faith is the substance of things hoped for, the evidence of things not seen.

Psalms 23:1-6 KJV :: The Lord is my shepherd; I shall not want. He maketh me to lie down in green pastures: he leadeth me beside the still waters. He restoreth my soul: he leadeth me in the paths of righteousness for his name's sake. Yea, though I walk through the valley of the shadow of death, I will fear no evil: for thou art with me; thy rod and thy staff they comfort me. Thou preparest a table before me in the presence of mine enemies: thou anointest my head with oil; my cup runneth over. Surely goodness and mercy shall follow me all the days of my life: and I will dwell in the house of the Lord forever.

Job 32:7-9 KJV :: I said, Days should speak, and multitude of years should teach wisdom. But there is a spirit in man: and the inspiration of the Almighty giveth them understanding. Great men are not always wise: neither do the aged understand judgment.

Proverbs 3:1-35 KJV :: My son, forget not my law; but let thine heart keep my commandments: For length of days, and long life, and peace, shall they add to thee. Let not mercy and truth forsake thee: bind them about thy neck; write them upon the table of thine heart: So shalt thou find favour and good understanding in the sight of God and man. Trust in the Lord with all thine heart; and lean not unto thine own understanding. In all thy ways acknowledge him, and he shall direct thy paths. Be not wise in thine own eyes: fear the Lord , and depart from evil. It shall be health to thy navel, and marrow to thy bones. Honour the Lord with thy substance, and with the firstfruits of all thine increase: So shall thy barns be filled with plenty, and thy presses shall burst out with new wine. My son, despise not the chastening of the Lord ; neither be weary of his correction: For whom the Lord loveth he correcteth; even as a father the son in whom he delighteth. Happy is the man that findeth wisdom, and the man that getteth understanding. For the merchandise of it is better than the merchandise of silver, and the gain thereof than fine gold. She is more precious than rubies: and all the things thou canst desire are not to be compared unto her. Length of days is in her right hand; and in her left hand riches and honour. Her ways are ways of pleasantness, and all her paths are peace. She is a tree of life to them that lay hold upon her: and happy is every one that retaineth her. The Lord by wisdom hath founded the earth; by understanding hath he established the heavens. By his knowledge the depths are broken up, and the clouds drop down the dew. My son, let not them depart from thine eyes: keep sound wisdom and discretion: So shall they be life unto thy soul, and grace to thy neck. Then shalt thou walk in thy way safely, and thy foot shall not stumble. When thou liest down, thou shalt not be afraid: yea, thou shalt lie down, and thy sleep shall be sweet. Be not afraid of sudden fear, neither of the desolation of the wicked, when it cometh. For the Lord shall be thy confidence, and shall keep thy foot from being taken. Withhold not good from them to whom it is due, when it is in the power of thine hand to do it. Say not unto thy neighbour, Go, and come again, and tomorrow I will give; when thou hast it by thee. Devise not evil against thy neighbour, seeing he dwelleth securely by thee. Strive not with a man without cause, if he have done thee no harm. Envy thou not the oppressor, and choose none of his ways. For the froward is abomination to the Lord : but his secret is with the righteous. The curse of the Lord is in the house of the wicked: but he blesseth the habitation of the just. Surely he scorneth the scorners: but he giveth grace unto the lowly. The wise shall inherit glory: but shame shall be the promotion of fools.

2) Understand Your Brand

James 2:14-26 KJV :: What doth it profit, my brethren, though a man say he hath faith, and have not works? can faith save him? If a brother or sister be naked, and destitute of daily food, And one of you say unto them, Depart in peace, be ye warmed and filled; notwithstanding ye give them not those things which are needful to the body; what doth it profit? Even so faith, if it hath not works, is dead, being alone. Yea, a man may say, Thou hast faith, and I have works: shew me thy faith without thy works, and I will shew thee my faith by my works. Thou believest that there is one God; thou doest well: the devils also believe, and tremble. But wilt thou know, O vain man, that faith without works is dead? Was not Abraham our father justified by works, when he had offered Isaac his son upon the altar? Seest thou how faith wrought with his works, and by works was faith made perfect? And the scripture was fulfilled which saith, Abraham believed God, and it was imputed unto him for righteousness: and he was called the Friend of God. Ye see then how that by works a man is justified, and not by faith only. Likewise also was not Rahab the harlot justified by works, when she had received the messengers, and had sent them out another way? For as the body without the spirit is dead, so faith without works is dead also.

3) write, Write, WRITE
Habakkuk 2:1-3 KJV :: I will stand upon my watch, and set me upon the tower, and will watch to see what he will say unto me, and what I shall answer when I am reproved. And the Lord answered me, and said, Write the vision, and make it plain upon tables, that he may run that readeth it. For the vision is yet for an appointed time, but at the end it shall speak, and not lie: though it tarry, wait for it; because it will surely come, it will not tarry.

4) Develop, Grow & Expand your Network
1 Chronicles 4:9-10 KJV :: And Jabez was more honourable than his brethren: and his mother called his name Jabez, saying, Because I bare him with sorrow. And Jabez called on the God of Israel, saying, Oh that thou wouldest bless me indeed, and enlarge my coast, and that thine hand might be with me, and that thou wouldest keep me from evil, that it may not grieve me! And God granted him that which he requested.

5) Be Professional in all you do
1 Corinthians 14:40 KJV :: Let all things be done decently and in order.

6) Build your "A" Team
Ecclesiastes 4:8-10 KJV :: There is one alone, and there is not a second; yea, he hath neither child nor brother: yet is there no end of all his labour; neither is his eye satisfied with riches; neither saith he, For whom do I labour, and bereave my soul of good? This is also vanity, yea, it is a sore travail. Two are better than one; because they have a good reward for their labour. For if they fall, the one will lift up his fellow: but woe to him that is alone when he falleth; for he hath not another to help him up.

7) Relationships
Philippians 2:4-5 KJV :: Look not every man on his own things, but every man also on the things of others. Let this mind be in you, which was also in Christ Jesus.

8) Execuie with Authority
Daniel 2:36-38 KJV :: This is the dream; and we will tell the interpretation thereof before the king. Thou, O king, art a king of kings: for the God of heaven hath given thee a kingdom, power, and strength, and glory. And wheresoever the children of men dwell, the beasts of the field and the fowls of the heaven hath he given into thine hand, and hath made thee ruler over them all. Thou art this head of gold.

Proverbs 29:1-3 KJV :: He, that being often reproved hardeneth his neck, shall suddenly be destroyed, and that without remedy. When the righteous are in authority, the people rejoice: but when the wicked beareth rule, the people mourn. Whoso loveth wisdom rejoiceth his father: but he that keepeth company with harlots spendeth his substance.

References:

1.1 **{Matthew 6:33 KJV}** But seek ye first the kingdom of God, and his righteousness; and all these things shall be added unto you.

1.2 **{1 Thessalonians 5:16-18 KJV}** Rejoice evermore. Pray without ceasing. In everything give thanks: for this is the will of God in Christ Jesus concerning you.

4. **{1 Corinthians 13:11 KJV}** :: When I was a child, I spake as a child, I understood as a child, I thought as a child: but when I became a man, I put away childish things.

7. "**The Gambler**" is a song written by Don Schlitz and recorded by American country music artist Kenny Rogers.

About the Author

Nicholas "Nick" Bartley, M.Ed is a serial entrepreneur with 15+ years of "qualified" experience in meeting/event planning, graphic design, brand management, and business development consultation. He brings a wealth of knowledge and experience that contribute to his success in fully grasping his client's vision. His experience includes planning regional/national conferences (with up to 10,000+ attendees), graphic design (logos, collateral and websites) for clients nationwide, managing a $65M college budget, sponsorship acquisition, image & professional development for high school students up to young professionals, and the list could go on. His unique background of education, financial management, customer focus principles, and innovative event planning & creative design experiences combine as an infusion of the perfect blend to accomplish his client's mission and goals for their respective project.

After building a solid five year career foundation working at Morehouse College, Nicholas decided to pursue this long awaited entrepreneurial endeavor...to own his own conference and special events planning & design company. In 2009 that dream was realized with a trust fall on faith that led to the formation of V2L Events, LLC (now The V2L Corporation, LLC), an event planning & management firm focused on highlighting the client's brand image through their events. By 2011 the demand shifted to branding & marketing and fostered the development of the V2L Design Studio. The founding vision and current practice is to make V2L a "one-stop" branding solutions firm to assist with event planning, branding & marketing, and business development in one seamless production package. Additionally, his commitment to assisting in business and entrepreneurial development led to creating The Entrepreneurial Cooperative (2012) and The 168 Life Project (2014).

Nicholas is a native of Savannah, Ga and is a product of the Chatham County Public School System completing the Business, Legal, Financial Magnet Program at the "historic" Savannah High School, he obtained a B.S. degree in Mathematics from Morehouse College, an M.Ed degree in Educational Leadership from Georgia State University, and a Certificate of Hospitality Administration in Trade Show and Event Planning from the J. Mack College of Business at Georgia State University. He served in professional capacities as Budget Assistant, Budget Analyst and Director of On-Campus Recruitment & Special Events all at Morehouse College prior to venturing into the entrepreneurial journey. Currently, he resides in Atlanta, Ga and is a proud member of Kappa Alpha Psi Fraternity, Inc and a devoted member at New Faith Mission Ministry (Griffin, Ga) where he serves on the Finance Team and is Director of Media & Marketing.

To review Nick's full Bio visit:
www.NickBartleyPresents.com

Connect with Nick on...
Facebook.com/V2Lceo
Instagram.com/V2Lceo
Twitter.com/V2Lceo
Periscope.tv/V2Lceo
Linkedin.com/in/nbartley